Kidstart

Name

Activity Book

Blended Math and Language Activities

triumphlearning™

Acknowledgments

Illustrations Constanza Basaluzzo (tl)iv, 1-4, (br)49, (tl, tc, bc)103; Shirley Beckes 29-30; Paige Billin-Frye 16, 69-70, 72-73; Hector Borlasca (tr, tl)49, 93-94, 104; Jan Bryant-Hunt 25, 27-28, (bl)103, 107; Mircea Causanu (br)iv, (br)v, 86; Chi Chung 66, 68; Laura Ferraro Close 41-42; Holli Conger 20; Sarah Dillard 37-39, 119; Laura Gonzalez 33, 35-36, (br)103; TSI Graphics 11-12, 26, 81-82, 105-106, 108; Melissa Iwai 50, (tr)120; Ian Joven (tr)v, 24; Colleen Madden (bl)49, 53-56, (cr, br)120; Julissa Mora 61, 63-64, 121-129; Mick Reid 57-60; Geoffrey Smith iii, 5-8, 51-52, 77-80, 83, (r)114, 133-137; Sarah Snow 17-18; MGabriele Tafuni 90; Mike Wesley 45.

Kidstart Activity Book, Math and English Language Arts, First Edition, Grade K   T001NA   ISBN-13: 978-1-62362-249-7

Triumph Learning® 136 Madison Avenue, 7th Floor, New York, NY 10016

Printed in the United States of America.   10 9 8 7 6

Contents

Lesson 1

Rhyming Counts! 1
Rhyme Time 3
Count to 10 and Rhyme Again! 4

Lesson 2

Plural Detectives 5
Count Along With Me 6
My Counting Book 7

Lesson 3

Letters Big and Small 9
Letters Big and Small 10
Alphabet Soup 11

Lesson 4

Ten Tens 13
Count by 10 15
Beginnings and Endings 16

Lesson 5

Then What Happened? 17
Count on Me 19
The Windy Day 20

Lesson 6

Spelling 21
Bunches of Bananas 23
What's Your Number? 24

Lesson 7

New Beginnings 25
Mystery Picture 26
This Way and That Way 27

Lesson 8

What Is 1 More? 29
Questions, Questions 31
Draw 1 More 32

Lesson 9

Soup for Friends 33
The Main Event 35
How Many? 36

Lesson 10

Dancing Puppets 37
Counting Animals 39
Animals in Motion 40

Lesson 11

Draw It 41

Details 42

Which Is More? 43

Which Is Less? 44

Lesson 12

Which Is More? 45

Compare Numbers 46

Number Puppets 47

Lesson 13

Different Sounds 49

Adding Letters 50

Add! 51

Lesson 14

Matching 53

Cross Them Out 54

Subtract! 55

Lesson 15

Tell It Again 57

How Many Hats? 59

Tell Me a Math Story 60

Lesson 16

The Three Little Pigs 61

Draw to Compare 62

How Many? 63

Lesson 17

Sharing Markers 65

What Makes 7? 67

How Do You Feel Today? 68

Lesson 18

Picking Apples 69

Ten in All 71

My Apple Fact 72

Lesson 19

What Can You Do? 73

Can You Add? 74

Can You Subtract? 75

Family Portrait 76

Lesson 20

How Many Ones? 77

Celebrate! 78

Fourth of July 79

Lesson 21

Growing Leaves 81

Winter Jobs, Summer Jobs 83

Helping Out 84

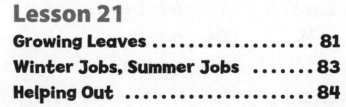

Lesson 22

My Favorite Animal 85

Tell About It 86

Draw It! 87

Lesson 23

Drawing Opposites 89

Compare It! 90

My Book of Opposites 91

Lesson 24

Animal Cards 93

My Sorting Chart 95

Sorting Mat 96

Lesson 25

What's My Position? 97

A House of Shapes 99

Listen and Draw 100

Lesson 26

Shape Up 101

How Many Syllables? 103

Find the Signs 104

Lesson 27

Flat or Solid? 105

Shapes in Sports 107

Does It Belong? 108

Lesson 28

Name That Shape 109

How Many Sides? 110

Shape Hunters 111

Lesson 29

I Learned 113

Solids in the Real World 114

Real-World Shapes 115

Lesson 30

I See Shapes 117

Write It Down 119

Let's Write 120

Picture Dictionary 121

The Alphabet 130

Uppercase Letters 131

Lowercase Letters 132

Colors 133

Flat Shapes.................... 134

Solid Shapes 135

1 and More Than 1 136

Find Their Homes 138

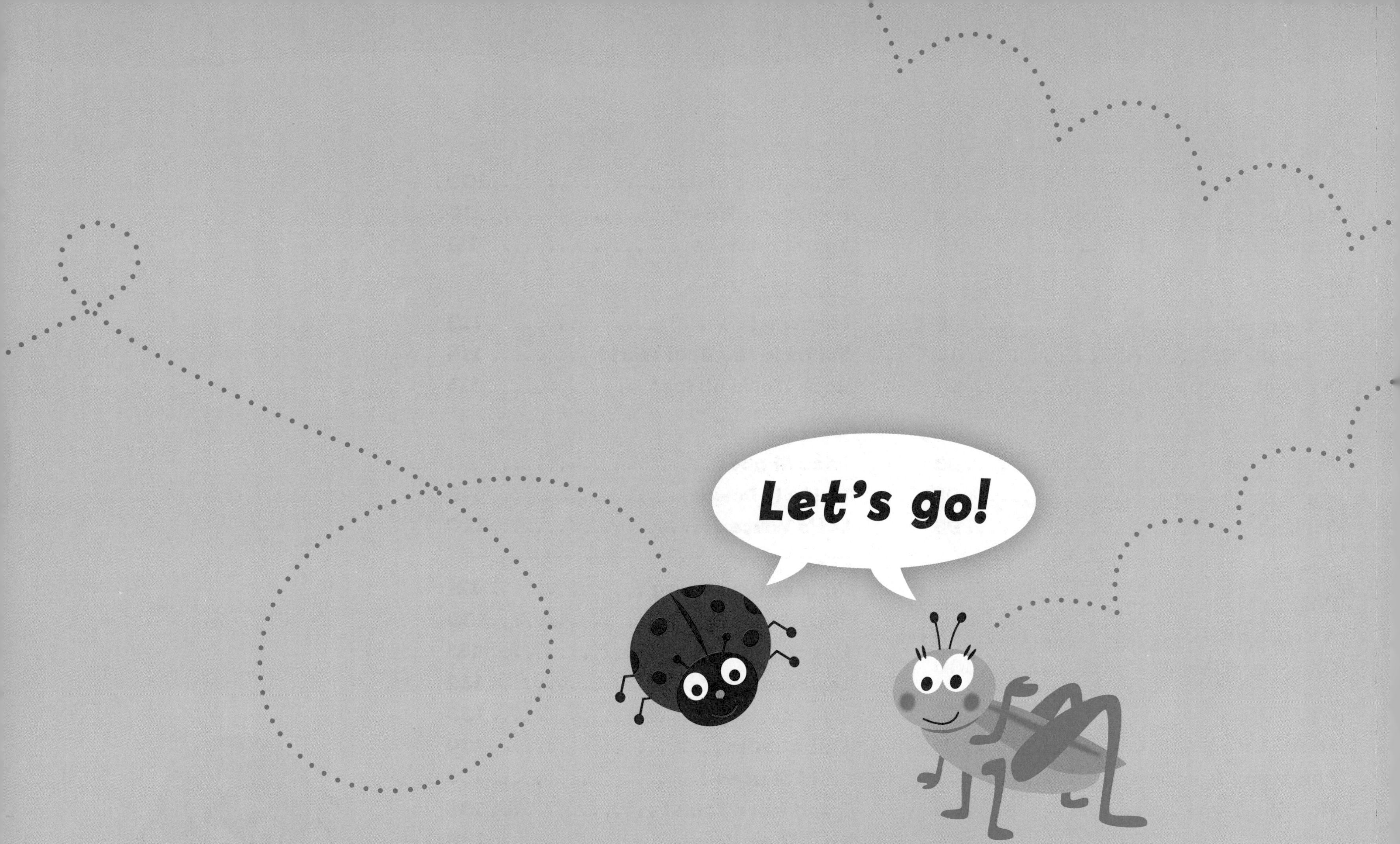
Let's go!

Rhyming Counts!

Name _____

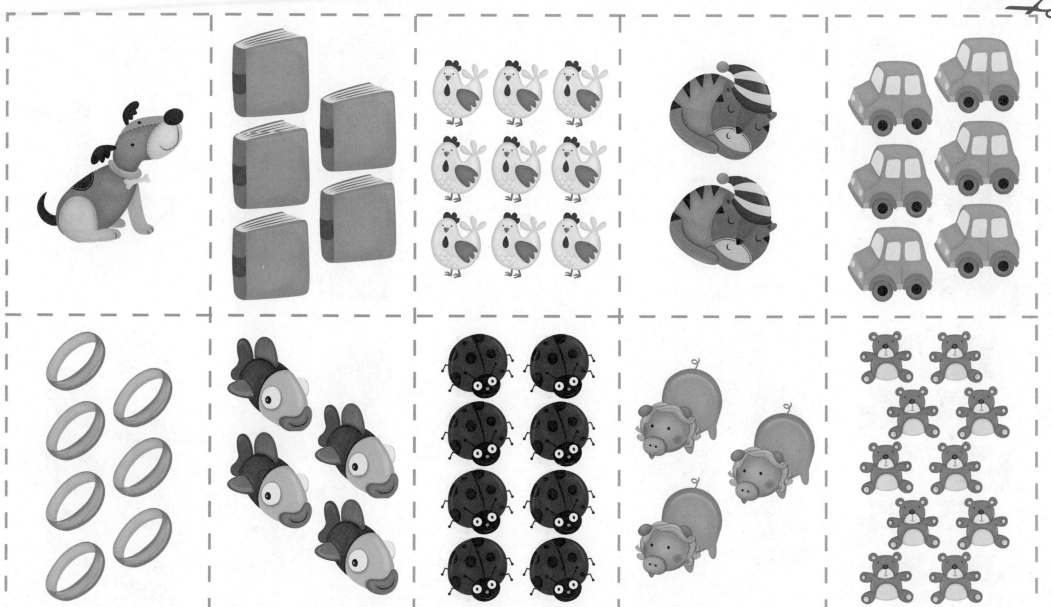

Directions Cut out the pictures.

1

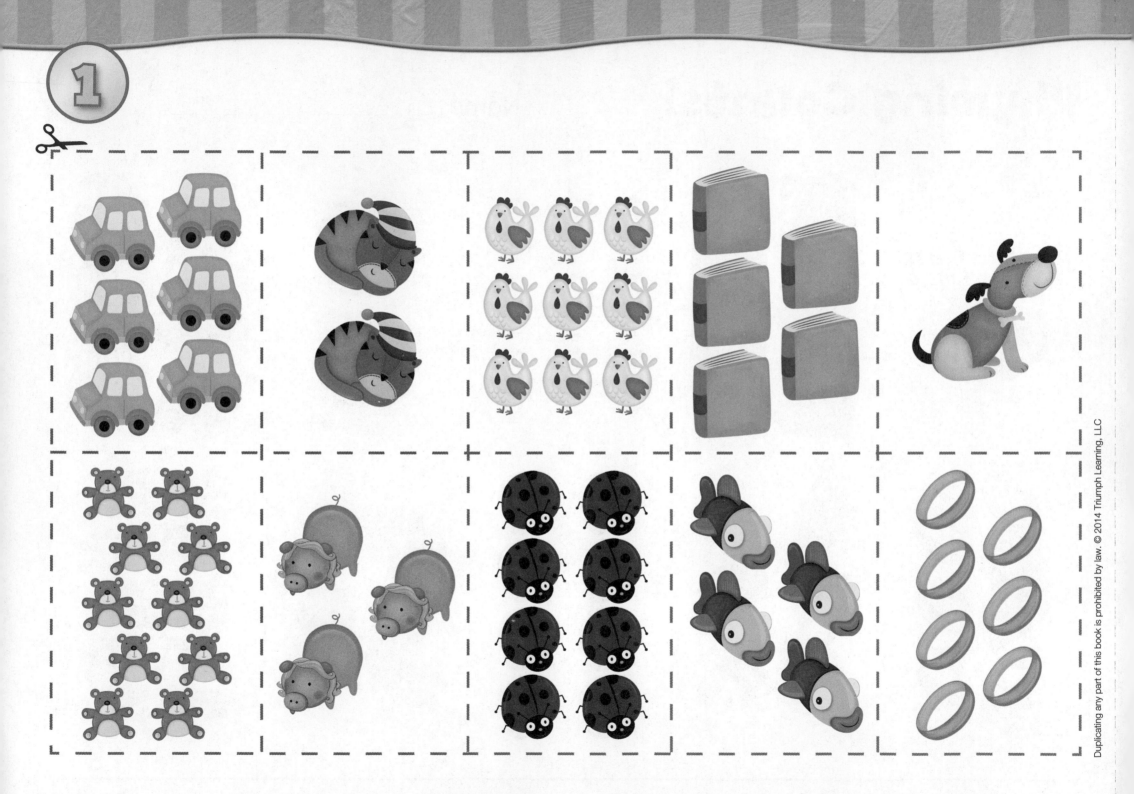

Rhyme Time

 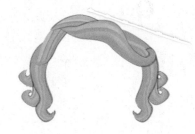  

Directions Name what each picture shows. Draw a line to match the pictures that rhyme.

Count to 10 and Rhyme Again!

Name _____

2

3

7

5

10

8

9

6

Directions Draw a line to connect the number of items to the correct numeral.

At Home Encourage children to count aloud. Have them say a rhyming word for each picture.

Plural Detectives

Name _____

 cub

 fox

 dog

 hen

dogs

cubs

hens

foxes

Directions Draw a line to match the singular noun to its plural form.
Then circle the letter or letters that make the word plural.

Count Along With Me

Name _____

       I count ▢ bug s .

    I count ▢ star s .

 I count ▢ bus es .

Directions Count and write the number of items. Then complete each sentence.

6

Name _____

My Counting Book

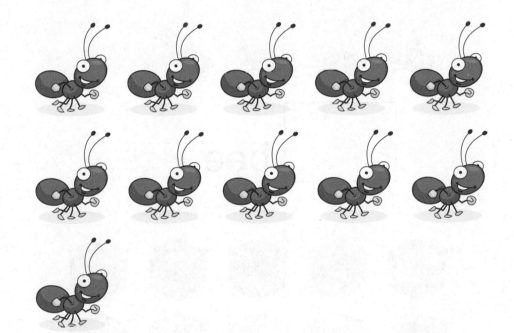

| | tree _____ |

| | ant 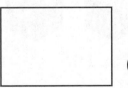 |

At Home Encourage children to read their books aloud. Then identify the letter or letters that make each word plural.

Directions Write the number and the plural form of the noun.

bee‾‾‾‾‾

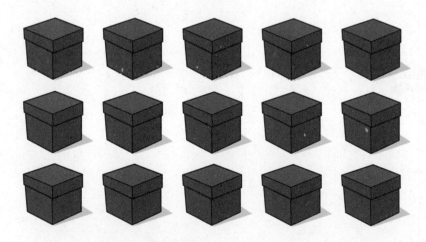

box‾‾‾‾

flower‾‾‾‾

Letters Big and Small

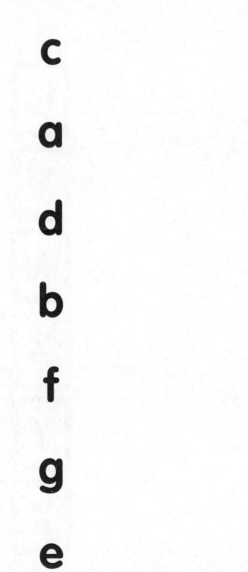

A
B
C
D
E
F
G

c
a
d
b
f
g
e

H
I
J
K
L
M

j
h
i
l
m
k

Directions Draw a line from the uppercase letter to its lowercase form.

At Home Have children use pages 9–10 to find and count the letters in their names.

Letters Big and Small

Name _____

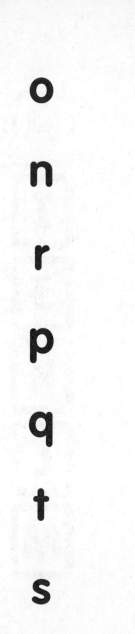

o
n
r
p
q
t
s

v
u
y
w
z
x

Directions Draw a line from the uppercase letter to its lowercase form.

Name _____

Alphabet Soup

Directions Color each uppercase letter blue and each lowercase letter green.

Duplicating any part of this book is prohibited by law. © 2014 Triumph Learning, LLC

Ten Tens

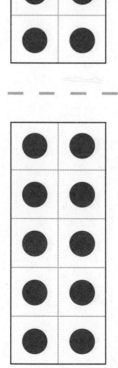
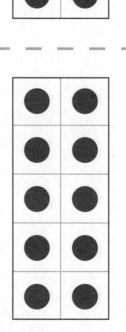
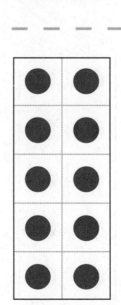

Directions Cut out the pictures.

Count by 10

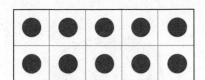 

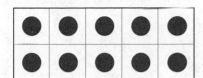

10   20   30

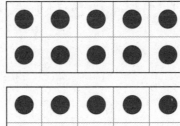

10   20   30

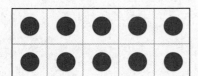 

20   30   40

20   30   40

Directions Use the ten frames to model counting by 10s.
Then circle the correct total.

4 Beginnings and Endings

F̶reddie and E̶ddy

T̶he boys count stickers __

_____

- -

_____

Directions Write each capital letter and place a period at the end of the sentence.

At Home Have children identify sentences in their favorite books.

Then What Happened?

Name _____

Directions Cut apart the illustrations from the story and order them.

Count On Me

Name _____

4

6

17

12

Directions Write the next three numbers in the boxes. On the last line, write any number other than 1, and then write the next three numbers.

5 The Windy Day

Name _____

Directions Write the numbers 1–4 to order the events shown in the pictures.

 At Home Encourage children to use the ordered illustrations to tell a story.

6

a e i o u l

n f g h c p

d b r s t m

Directions Cut apart the letters.

l u o i e a

p c h g f n

m t s r b d

Bunches of Bananas

Name _____

1. I see 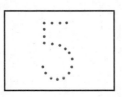 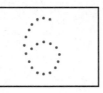 .

2. I see 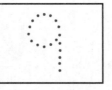 .

3. I see  .

4. I see .

Directions Draw the number of bananas named in each sentence.

At Home Encourage children to read their completed sentences aloud.

6 What's Your Number?

Name _____

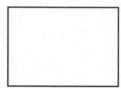

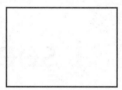

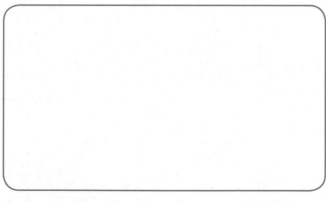

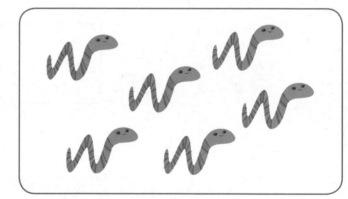

Directions Count the number of items shown in each illustration and write the number.

New Beginnings

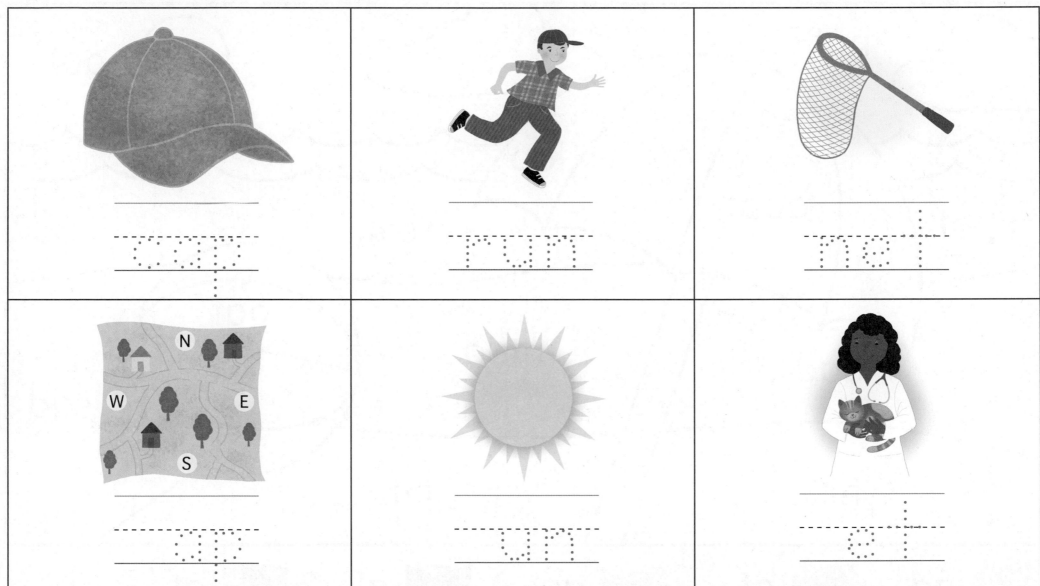

cap

run

net

ap

un

et

Directions Trace the letters. Then write the letter for the beginning sound of the word.

 At Home Encourage children to read word-family books at home with a family member.

Mystery Picture

Name _____

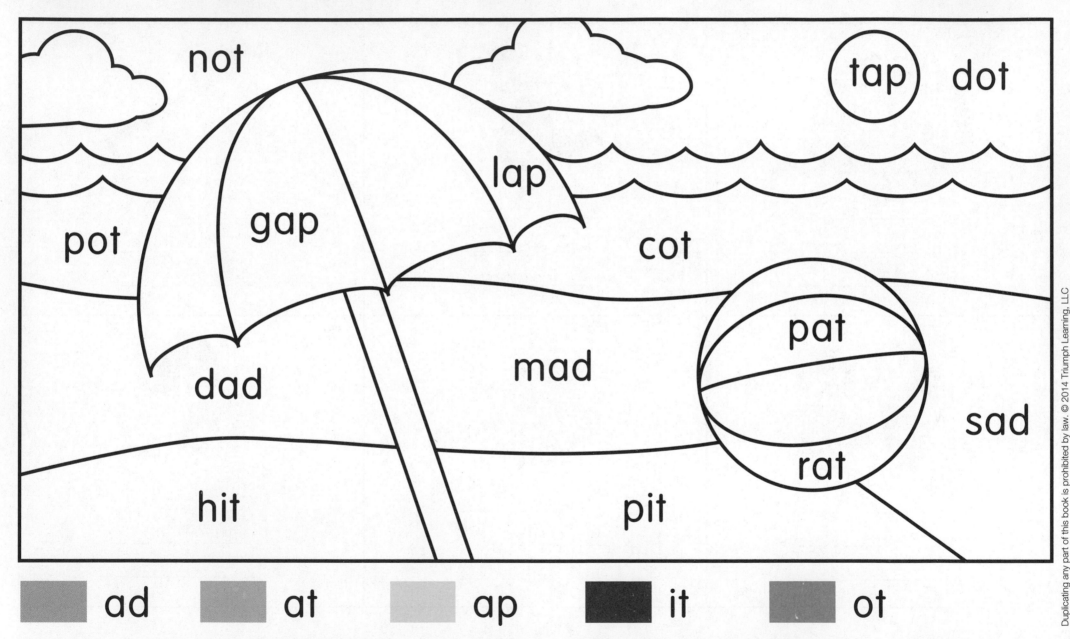

ad	at	ap	it	ot

Directions Color the word families to reveal a hidden picture.

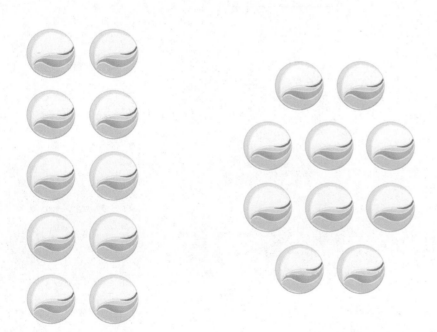

marbles

Name _____

This Way and That Way

apples

Directions Circle groups that show the same number of items.

[   ] cars

[   ] flowers

What Is 1 More?

Name _____

Directions Cut out the illustrations.

Questions, Questions

Name _____

1. <u>What</u> games does he play?

2. <u>Where</u> does he play?

3. <u>Who</u> plays with Benny?

Directions Write the question word to complete the sentence.

Draw 1 More

Name _____

Directions Draw to show one more circle than shown in each group.

At Home Encourage children to count groups of objects at home and then tell how many is one more.

What does Rabbit make?

Soup for Friends

Directions Circle the question word and underline the question mark. Then write or draw the answer.

Where is Rabbit?

What does Rabbit need?

The Main Event

Name _____

Directions Draw a picture to show the main event of "Soup for Friends." Use the picture to discuss the story.

 At Home Encourage children to use their pictures as they retell and act out the story.

How Many?

Name _____

1. How many  ?

2. How many  ?

3. How many  ?

Directions Count the objects and write how many.

Dancing Puppets

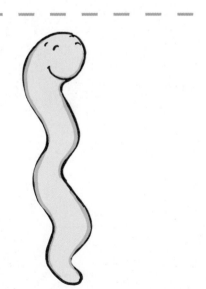

Directions Cut out the illustrations and use them to make stick puppets.
Use the puppets to demonstrate the action words in the poem.

Counting Animals

Name _____

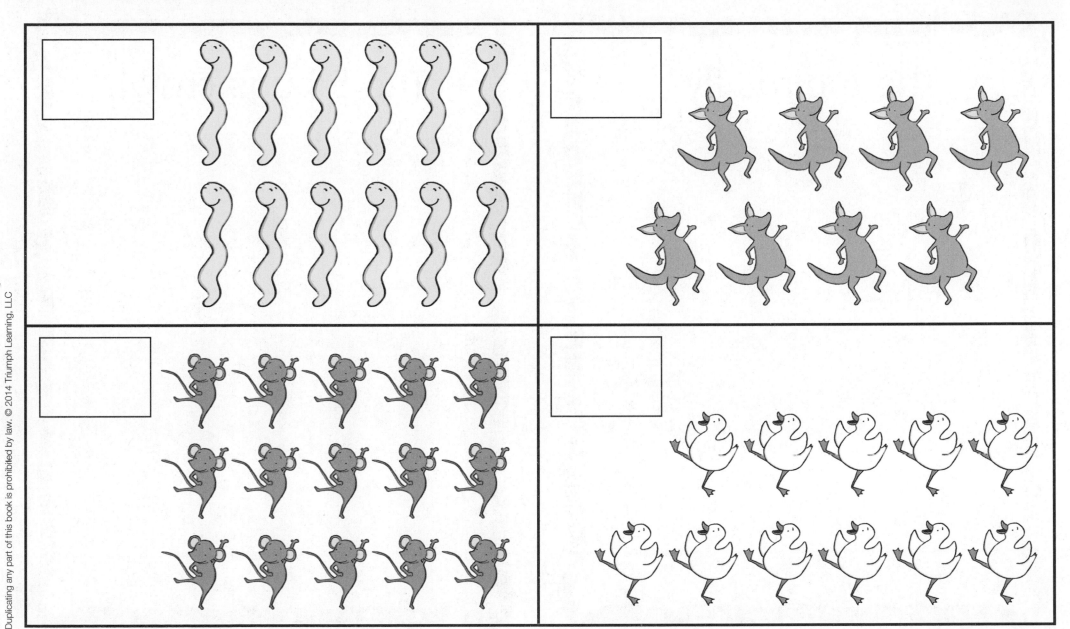

Directions Count the number of animals in each illustration.
Then tell how each animal moves.

Animals in Motion

Name _____

The 6 birds fly.

The 5 bugs crawl.

Directions Circle the verb. Draw a picture to show the action in each sentence.

 At Home Encourage children to act out and discuss different ways to move.

Draw It

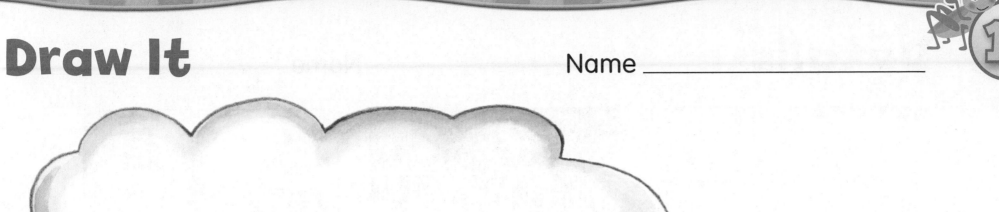

Directions Draw pictures of Miguel and Carmen's dreams. Share and talk about the pictures with the class.

Details

Name _____

Directions Circle the picture in each row that shows a detail from the story.
Then write a sentence about one of the details you circled.

Which Is More?

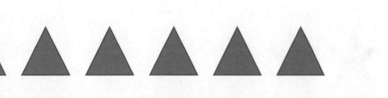

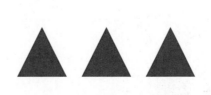

Directions Circle the group in each section that has more objects.

11

Which Is Less?

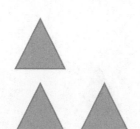

Directions Circle the group in each section that has fewer objects.

🏠 **At Home** Encourage children to compare groups of objects using the terms *greater than*, *less than*, or *equal to*.

Name _____

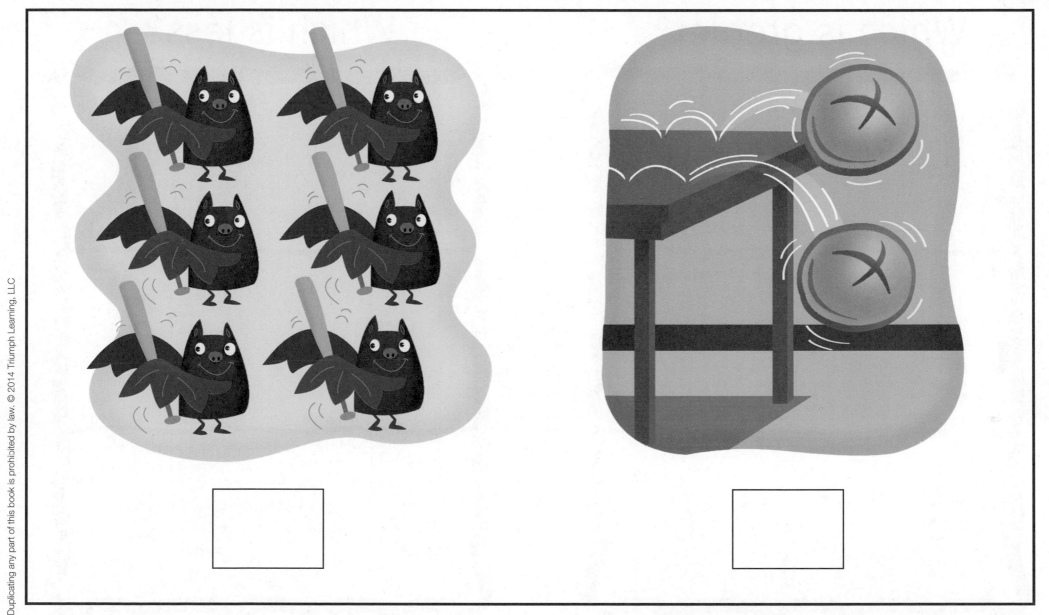

Directions Write the correct number in the space provided.
Then circle the greater number.

 At Home Encourage children to tell an adult a favorite
multiple-meaning word and explain why they like it.

Compare Numbers

Name _____

Which is greater?

4	3
2	8
5	6

Which is less?

6	5
10	9
7	8

Directions In the first column, circle the numbers that are greater.
In the second column, circle the numbers that are less.

Number Puppets

Name _____

1 2 3 4 5

6 7 8 9 10

Directions Cut apart the numbers. Then make stick puppets from the cutouts.

Different Sounds

Directions Say the name of each picture. Color the box with the sound that is different.

Adding Letters

Name _____

up		___ up
at		___ at
ox		___ ox

Directions Read the word in the first column. Then use the picture in the second column as a clue for adding a beginning letter to make a new word.

Draw 4 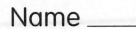.

Draw I more.

How many in all?

[ ] + [ ] = [ ]

 **At Home** Have children show an adult at home how to use drawings or objects to show addition.

Add!

Draw 3 .

Draw I more.

How many in all?

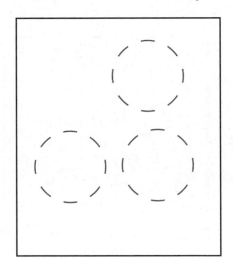 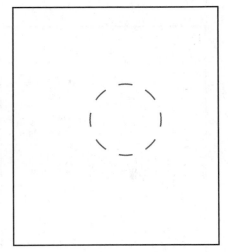

3 + I = [ ]

Directions Draw to find how many in all. Then fill in the equation.

51

Draw 2 .

Draw 2 more.

How many in all?

Draw 3 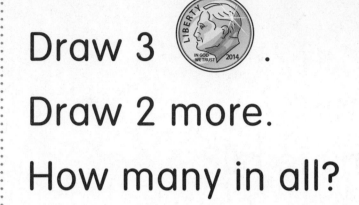.

Draw 2 more.

How many in all?

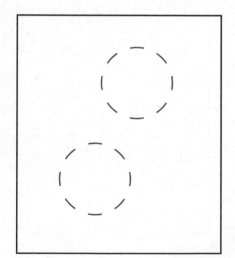 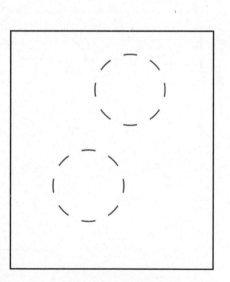

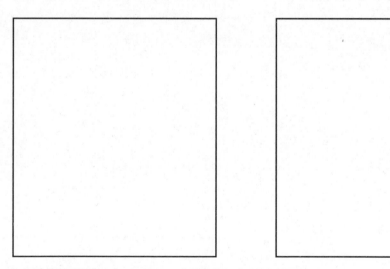

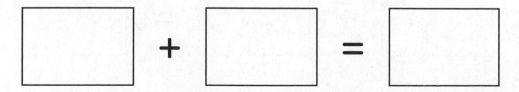

[ ] + [ ] = [ ]

[ ] + [ ] = [ ]

Matching

cup

net

pan

pin

bus

mat

Directions Match each picture with the corresponding word.

 At Home Encourage children to think of other words. Have them drop the initial letter-sound to see if they can make a new word.

53

Cross Them Out

Name _____

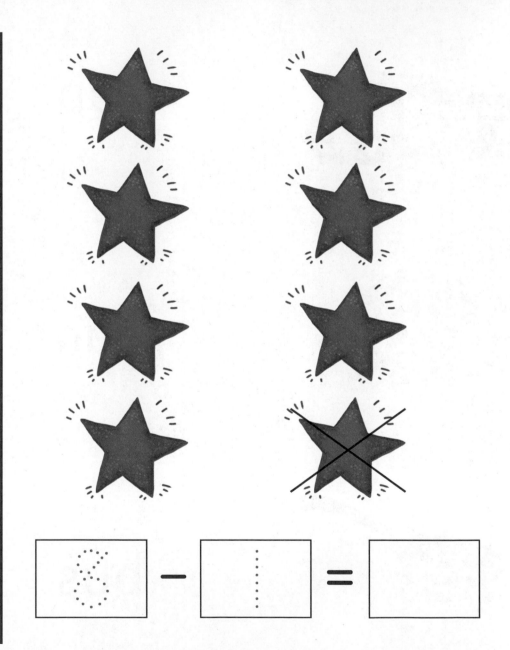

Directions Count the total number of items. Count the items that are crossed out.
Then complete the equation.

Name _____

Subtract!

☐ − ☐ = ☐

Directions Use each picture to complete the subtraction equations. Then make your own equation.

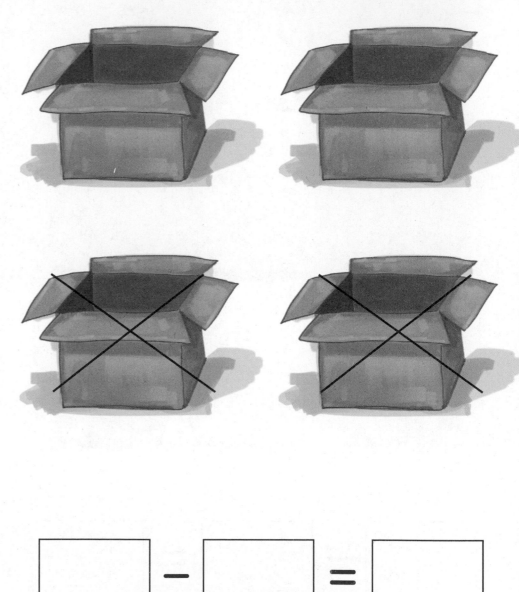

$$\boxed{} - \boxed{} = \boxed{}$$

$$\boxed{} - \boxed{} = \boxed{}$$

Tell It Again

Name _____

Directions Cut apart the pictures and use them to tell about the story.

How Many Hats?

Name _____

Pig has ☐ hats.

_____ has ☐ hats.

☐ + ☐ = ☐

They have ☐ hats.

Directions Write each word and count the number of hats.
Then write the numbers to complete the equation.

59

Tell Me a Math Story

Name _____

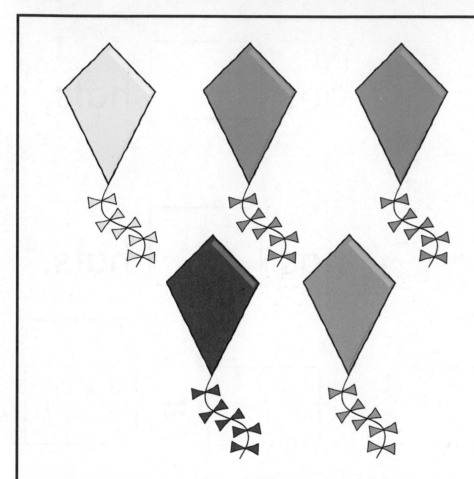

$$5 + \boxed{} = \boxed{}$$

Directions Draw a picture to show an addition word problem.
Use the drawing to complete the equation.

At Home Have children use their drawings to tell a story to an adult at home.

Name _____

Directions Number the pictures from the story in the order that they happened.

16 # Draw To Compare

Name _____

Directions Draw a character from each story. Then label each drawing.

 At Home Have children use their drawings to compare the characters for an adult at home.

$$\boxed{} - 1 = 2$$

Name _____

How Many?

$$10 - 4 = \boxed{}$$

Directions Cross out to show the subtraction. Then complete the equation.

7 - 5 = ▢

6 - ▢ = 4

Sharing Markers

Name _____

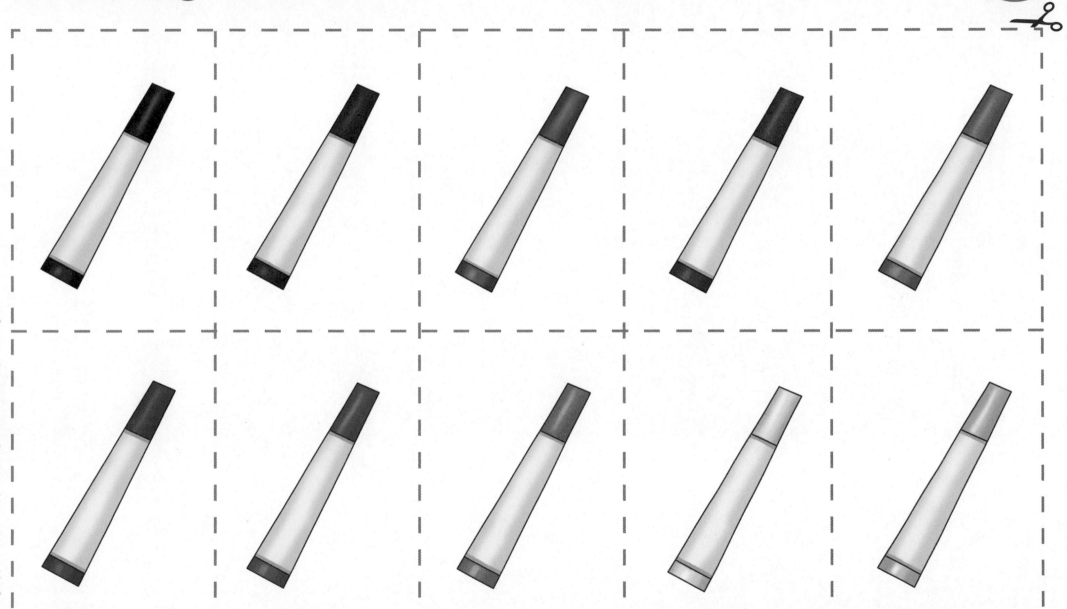

Directions Cut apart the pictures and use them to show ways to break apart numbers.

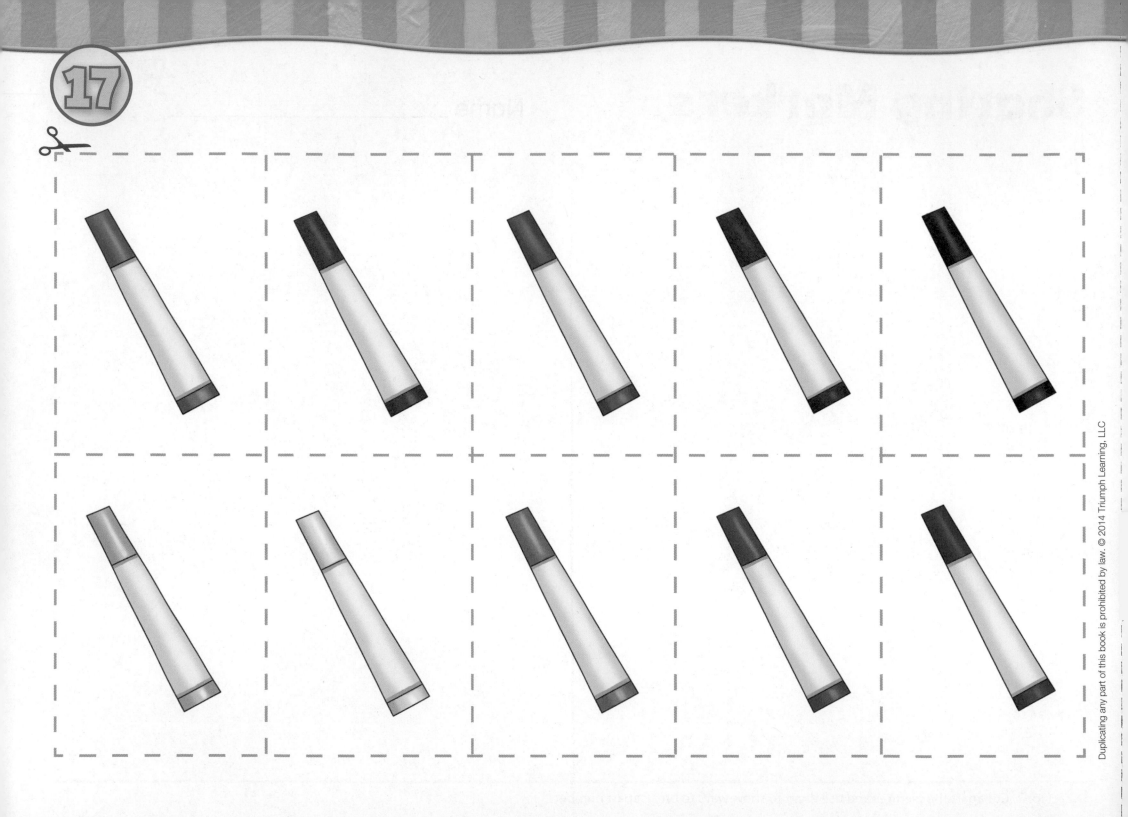

What Makes 7?

Name _____

$7 = 4 + \boxed{}$

$7 = 1 + \boxed{}$

$7 = \boxed{} + \boxed{}$

$7 = \boxed{} + \boxed{}$

Directions Use the counters to find different ways to make 7.

How Do You Feel Today?

Name _____

I feel _____

_____

Directions Draw a picture and write a sentence to tell a story about emotions.

 At Home Have children use their drawings as they retell their stories about feelings.

Picking Apples

Name _____

Directions Color the apples on page 69 red, and the apples on
page 70 yellow. Then cut out each shape.

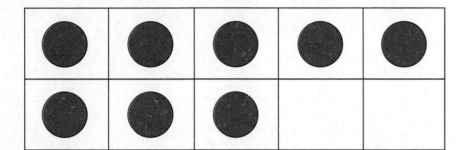

$$10 = 8 +$$ ☐

$$10 = 5 +$$ ☐

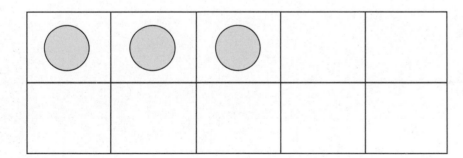

$$10 = 3 +$$ ☐

$$10 = 6 +$$ ☐

Directions Use the models to find the number that makes 10.
Then write the missing number to complete the equation.

18 My Apple Fact

Name _____

_____

- -

_____

- -

_____

Directions Draw a picture to show a fact about apples.
Then write a sentence to tell about the fact.

At Home Have children use their drawings to share apple facts they learned.

What Can You Do?

1. When I was I, I learned to _____ talk _____.

2. When I was 2, I learned to _____ run _____.

3. When I was 3, I learned to _____ throw _____.

4. When I was 4, I learned to _____ bike _____.

5. When I was 5, I learned to _____ add _____.

Directions Trace the word to complete each sentence.

Name _____

$3 + 2 =$ ☐ $2 + 1 =$ ☐

$1 + 1 =$ ☐ $1 + 4 =$ ☐

$2 + 2 =$ ☐ $3 + 0 =$ ☐

Directions Complete the addition equations.

Can You Subtract?

Name _____

5 − 3 = ☐

5 − 4 = ☐

4 − 1 = ☐

4 − 2 = ☐

3 − 2 = ☐

2 − 1 = ☐

Directions Complete the subtraction equations.

At Home Have children play a simple addition and subtraction game using pennies to add and subtract within 5.

19 Family Portrait

Name _____

My _____ is _____.

Directions Draw a picture of a family member. Then complete the sentence.

How Many Ones?

Name _____

$12 = 10 +$ ☐

$14 = 10 +$ ☐

Directions Count to find how many more ones are needed to make the number.

At Home Have children model how to break a number from 11 to 19 into one group of ten ones and some more ones.

Celebrate!

Name _____

_____

- -

_____

Directions Draw and write about a celebration.

Name _____

Fourth of July

parade

Directions Draw and label Fourth of July customs.

20

Growing Leaves

Name _____

Directions Cut out the tree and the leaves.

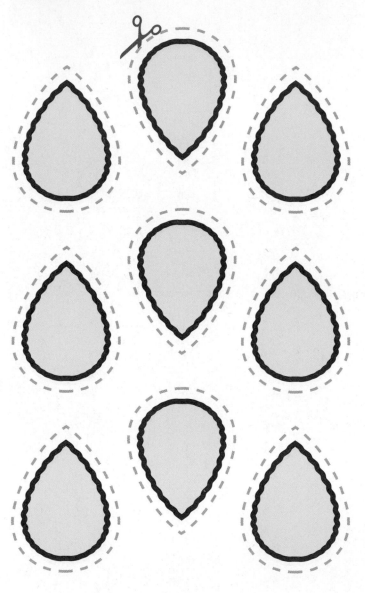

Winter Jobs, Summer Jobs

Name _____

Winter

Summer

Directions Trace the words at the top of the page.
Then circle two jobs that are usually done during that season.

Helping Out

Name _____

Directions Draw a picture about helping out at home.

At Home Have children use their drawings to show how they help out around the house.

My Favorite Animal

Name _____

My favorite animal is a _____.

Directions Draw a picture of your favorite animal.
Then complete the sentence.

 At Home Have children use their picture to tell about their favorite animal.

Tell about It

Name _____

Directions Circle the appropriate drawing after hearing the prompts.

short

Name _____

Draw It!

long

Directions Draw and write an example of an object that has the characteristic listed on each page.

heavy

light

_____

- - - - - - - - - - - - - - - - -

_____

_____

- - - - - - - - - - - - - - - - -

_____

Drawing Opposites

Name _____

Directions Draw and label a pair of opposites.

Compare It!

Name _____

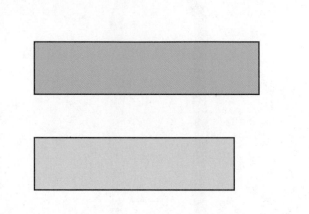

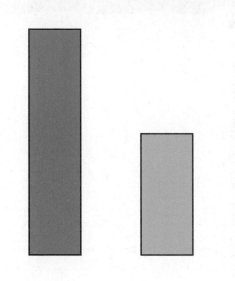

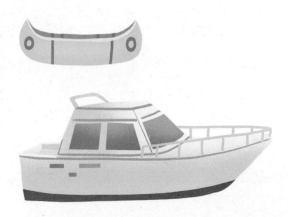

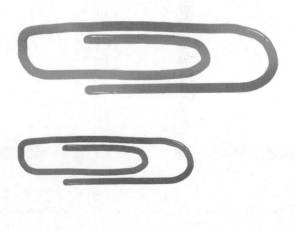

Directions Circle the appropriate picture after listening to the prompts.

 At Home Have children bring in two objects that can be compared to share with the class.

short

tall

Name _____

My Book of Opposites

big

small

Directions Draw and label a pair of opposites on each book page.

light

cold

heavy

hot

Animal Cards

Name _____

Directions Cut out the animal cards.

My Sorting Chart

Name _____

Fly	Walk	S̈ẅïm̈
☐	☐	☐

Directions Sort the animal cards using the categories.
Then count the animals in each category and write the number.

Sorting Mat

Name _____

Directions Use this page to practice sorting.

Duplicating any part of this book is prohibited by law. © 2014 Triumph Learning, LLC

 At Home Encourage children to use the mat to compare and sort different categories of items.

What's My Position?

Name _____

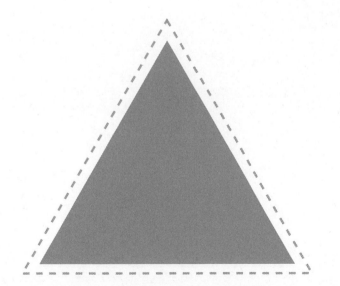

Directions Cut out the shapes.

At Home Have children use the shapes to talk about and demonstrate position words.

A House of Shapes

Name _____

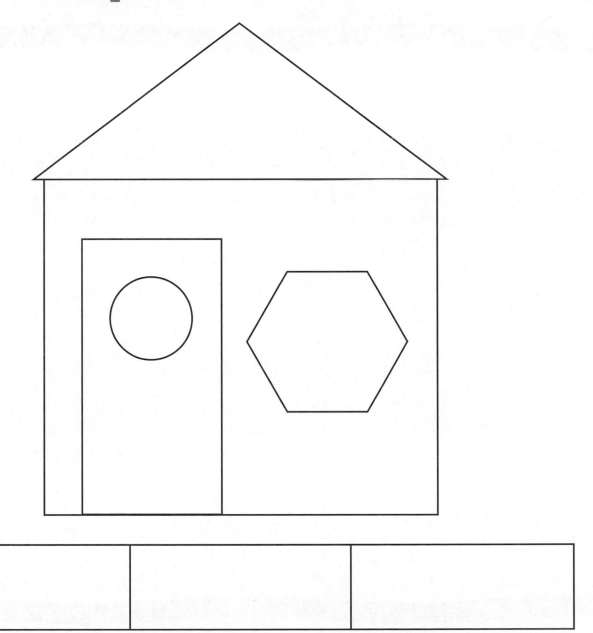

Directions Color the shapes based on the descriptions you hear.

Listen and Draw

Name _____

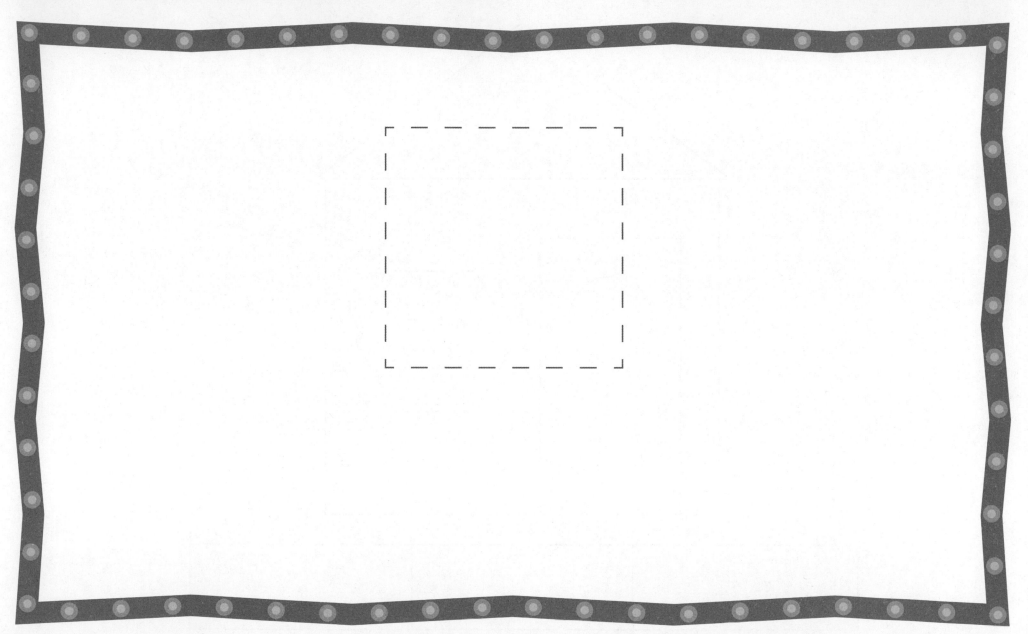

Directions Follow directions to draw a picture.

Shape Up

Name _____

Directions Color, then cut apart the shapes.

How Many Syllables?

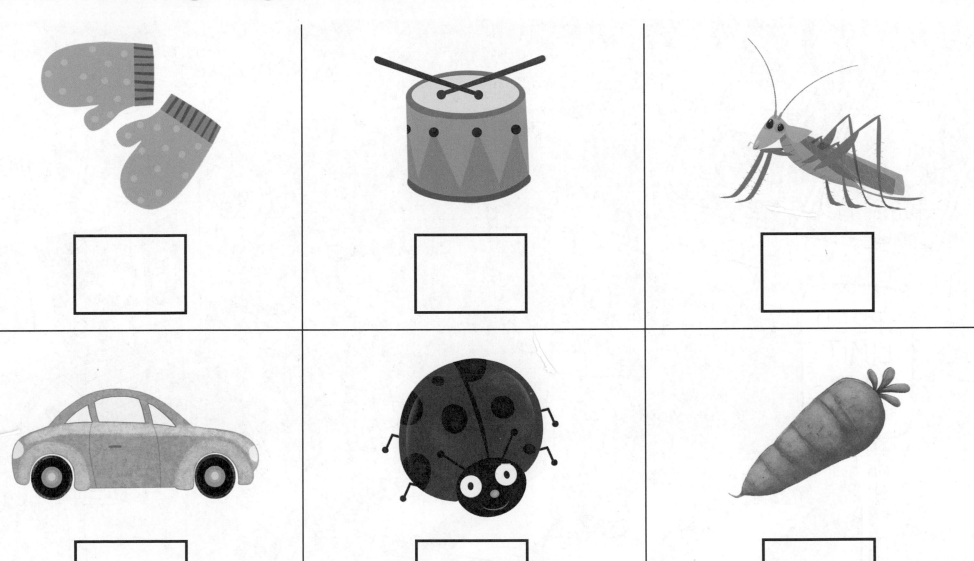

Directions Say the name of the picture. Then count the number of syllables in the word.
Write the number of syllables in the box.

26 Find the Signs

Name _____

Directions Circle the street signs in the picture.

 At Home Encourage children to explain the meaning of each street sign in the picture. Then discuss the meaning of street signs in your neighborhood.

Flat or Solid?

Name _____

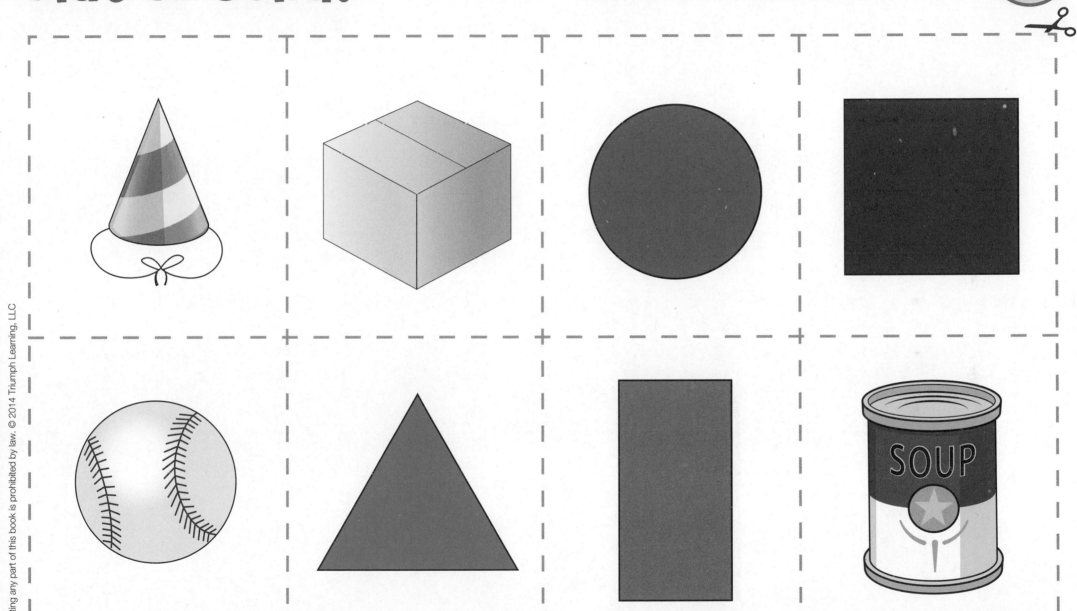

Directions Cut out the shapes along the dotted lines.

Shapes in Sports

Name _____

Directions Write a sentence to tell about each picture.

Does It Belong?

Name _____

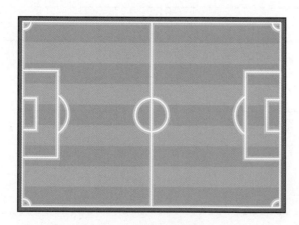
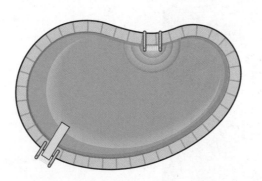
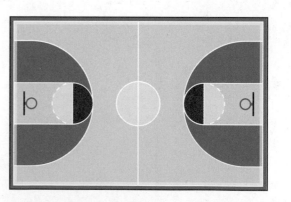

Directions Circle the pictures that have the same shape.

 At Home Encourage children to find examples of flat and solid shapes at home.

Name That Shape

Name _____

_____

What shape is the top of a cylinder ----------- _____

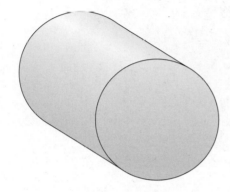

_____

What shape is the side of a cube ----------- _____

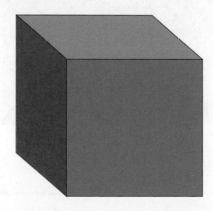

Directions Circle the question word and insert a question mark for each question.
Then draw to answer each question.

How Many Sides?

Name _____

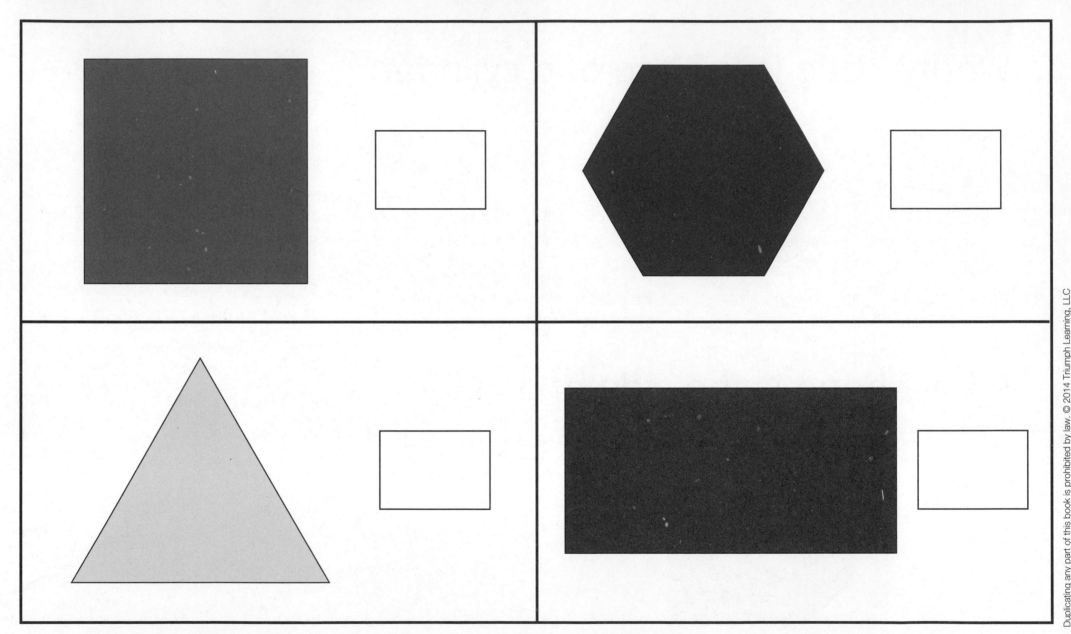

Directions Count the number of sides for each shape
and write the number in the space provided.

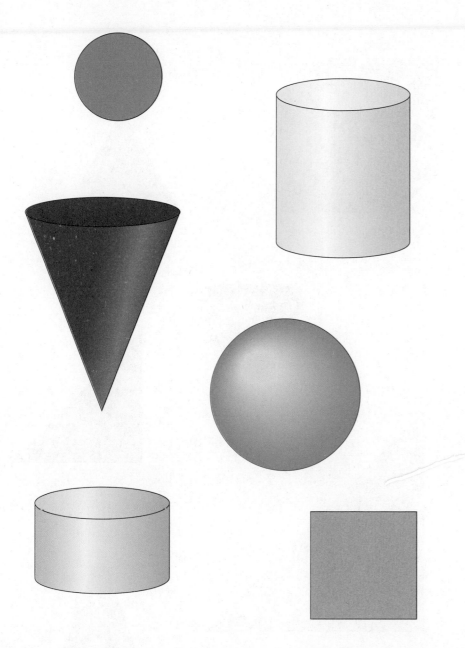

Name _____

Shape Hunters

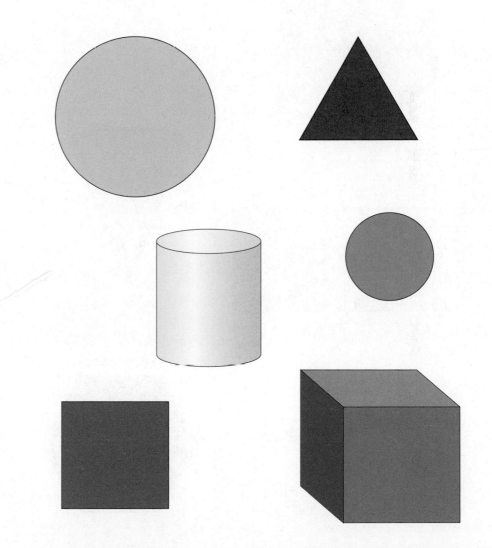

At Home Have children tell how the shapes are alike and different.

Directions Listen to the directions and circle the correct shapes.

III

I Learned . . .

Directions Draw a picture and write a sentence about something you learned in the text.

Solids in the Real World

Name _____

Directions Match each shape with the correct picture.

Name _____

Real-World Shapes

At Home Have children use their drawings to talk about examples of geometric solid shapes in the real world.

Directions Draw a real-world object that has the same shape as the one shown.

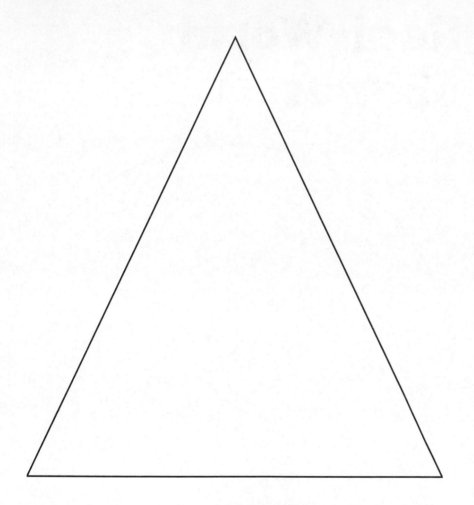

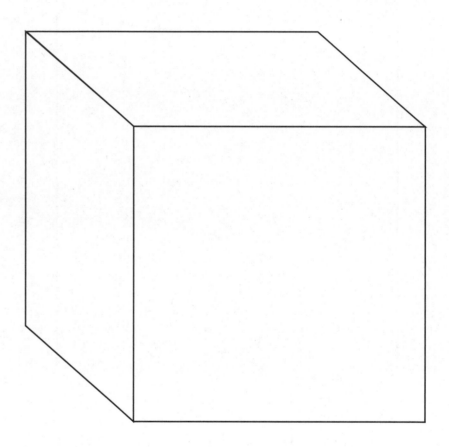

I See Shapes

Name _____

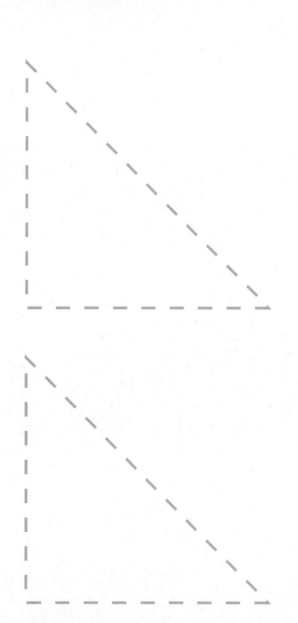

Directions Color and then cut out the shapes.

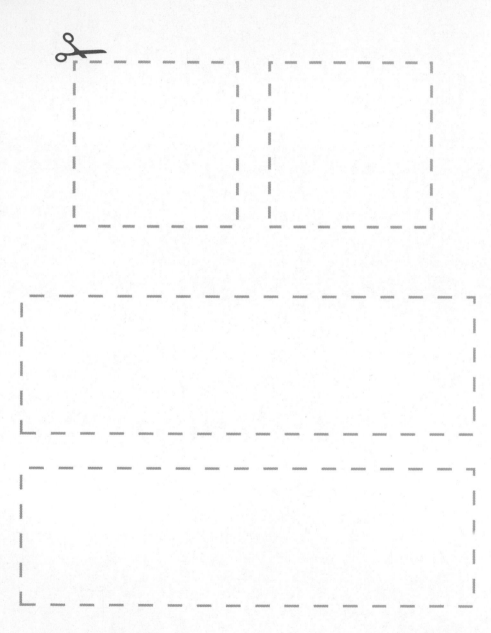

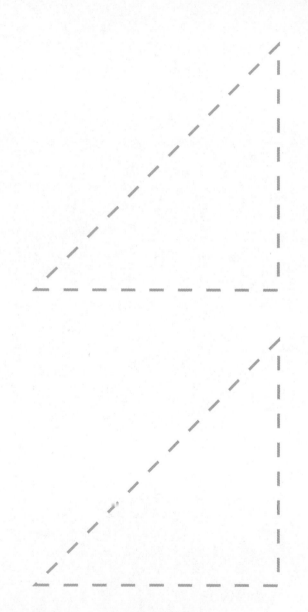

Write It Down

1. I see the cat _____

2. What do we do _____

3. We have a dog _____

Directions Listen to the sentence and write the correct end punctuation.

 At Home Have children tell a story to an adult at home.

Let's Write

Name _____

1. _____ see the _____ .

2. _____ see the _____ .

3. _____ see the _____ .

Directions Complete each sentence.

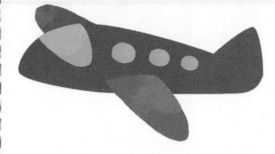

Picture Dictionary

A House

 bed

 blanket

 bowl

 door

 lamp

 milk

 soap

 spoon

 table

 toothbrush

A Classroom

 backpack

 glue

 book

 paper

 chair

 pencil

 computer

 rug

 crayon

 teacher

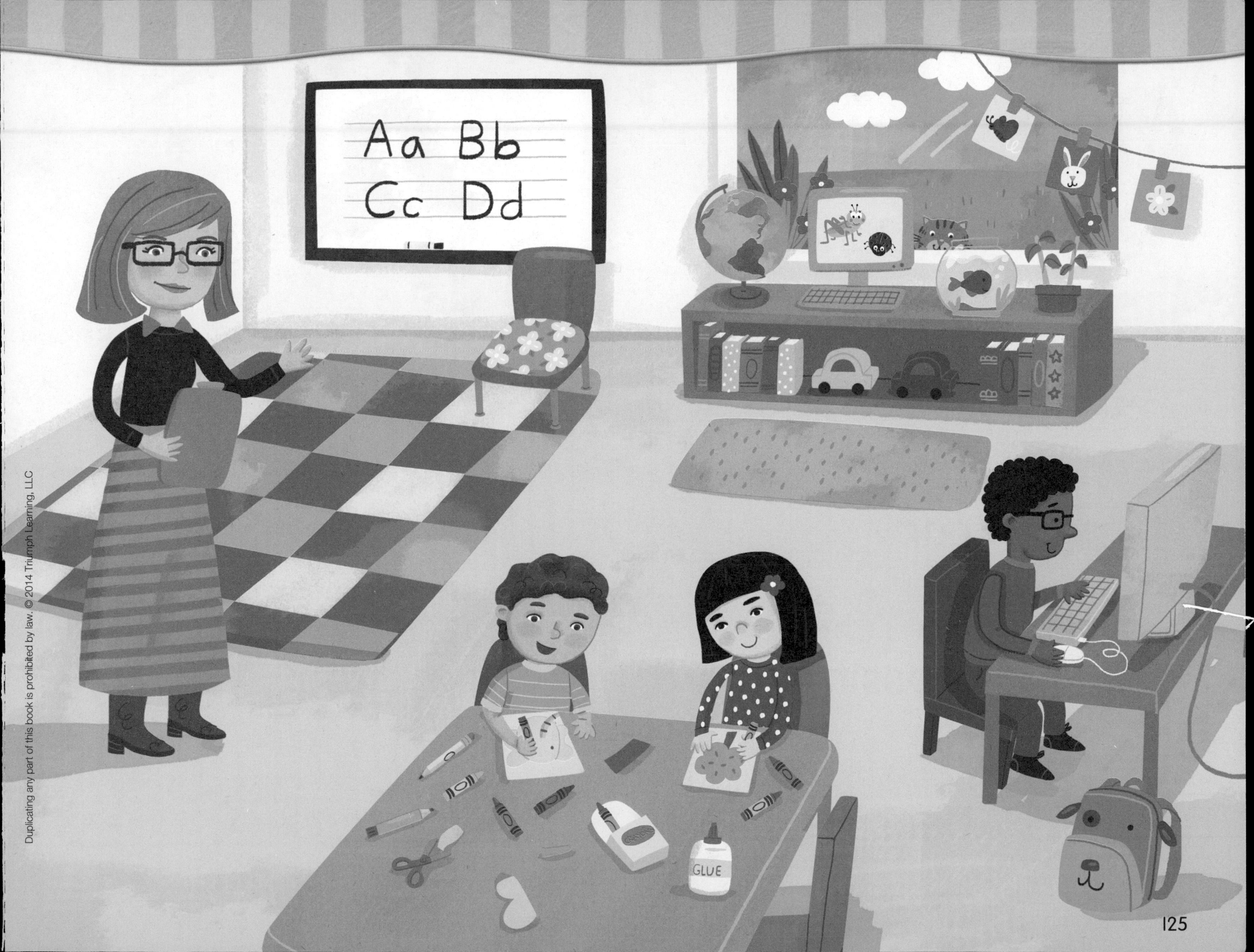
Aa Bb
Cc Dd
GLUE

A Town

 airplane

 bus

 car

 crossing guard

 house

 stop sign

 street

 streetlight

 tree

 truck

A Farm

 barn

 girl

 cloud

 grass

 corn

 horse

 duck

 pig

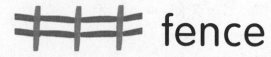 fence

sun

The Alphabet

Aa Bb Cc Dd Ee Ff

Gg Hh Ii Jj Kk Ll

Mm Nn Oo Pp Qq

Rr Ss Tt Uu Vv

Ww Xx Yy Zz

Uppercase Letters

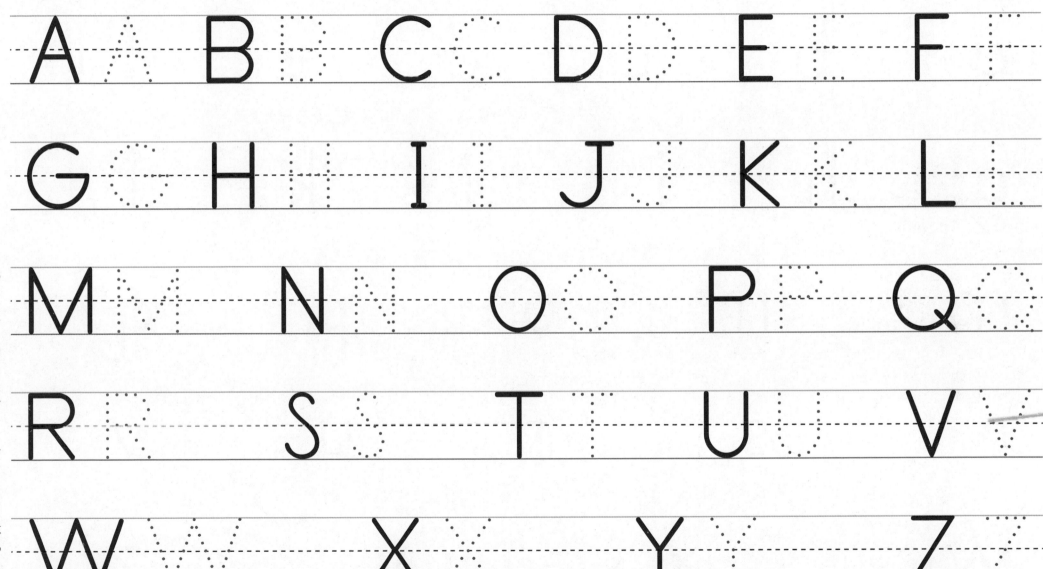

Lowercase Letters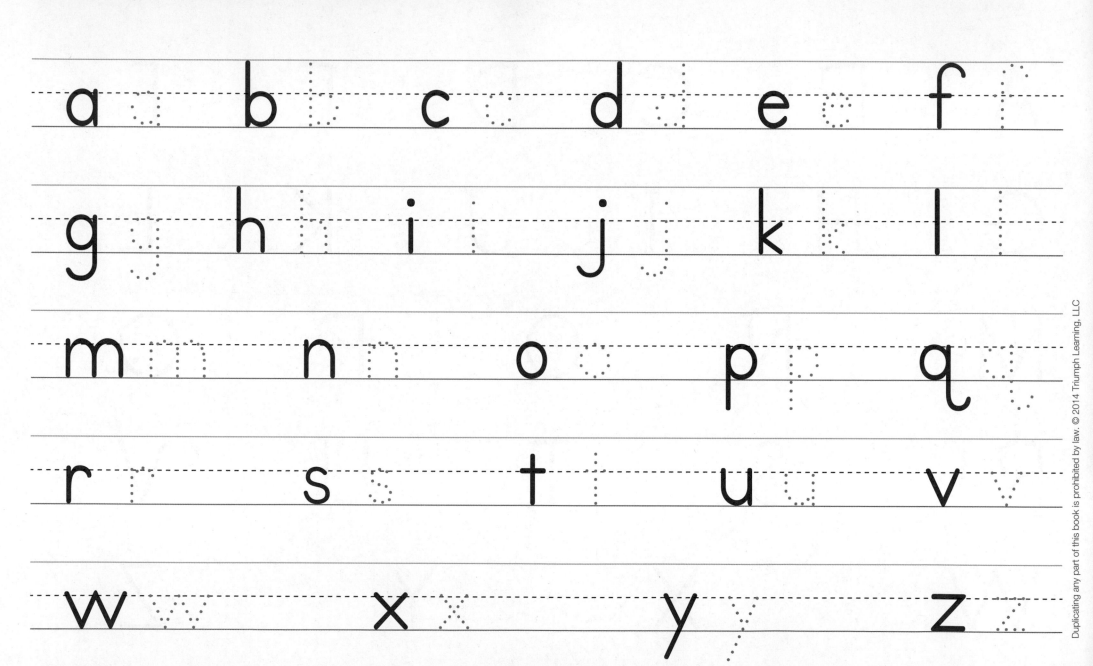

a   b   c   d   e   f

g   h   i   j   k   l

m   n   o   p   q

r   s   t   u   v

w   x   y   z

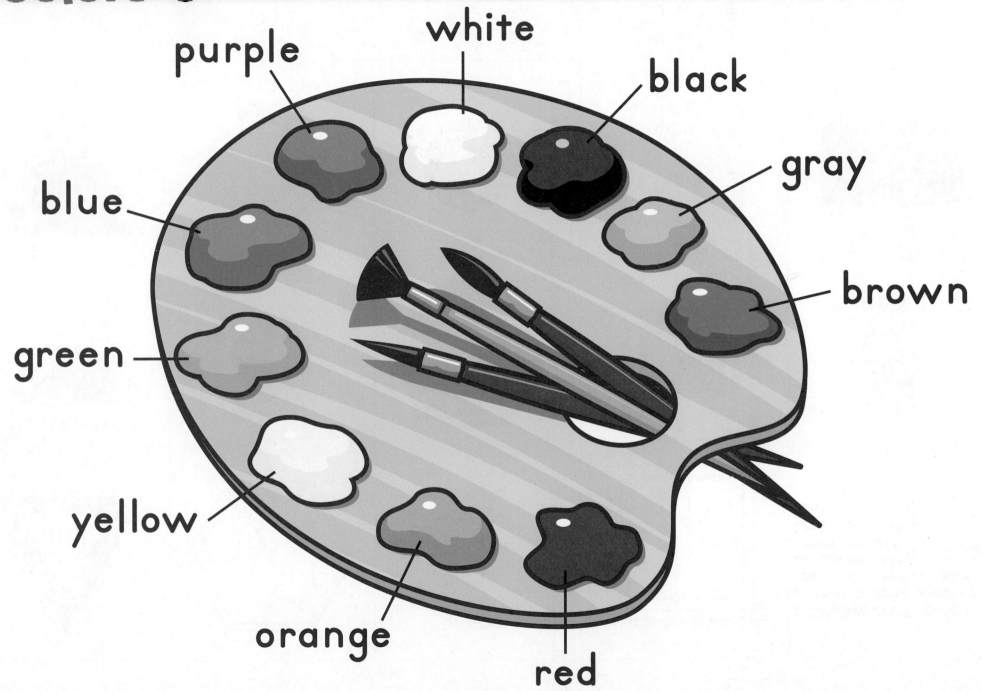

purple

white

black

gray

blue

brown

green

yellow

orange

red

Flat Shapes

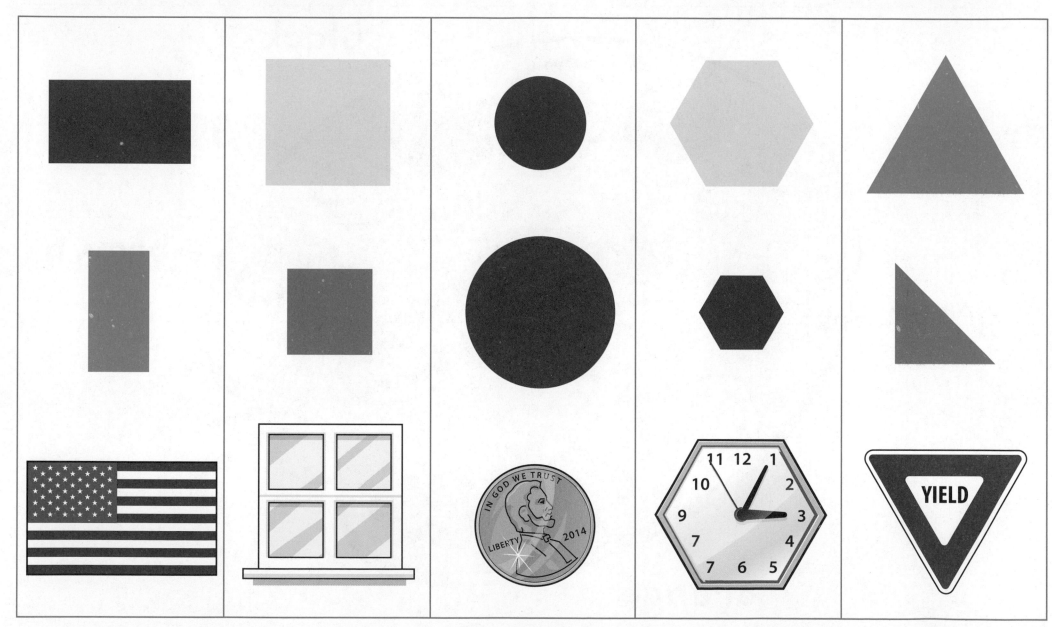

Solid Shapes

🐝 1 and More Than 1

 1 panda

 2 pandas

 1 car

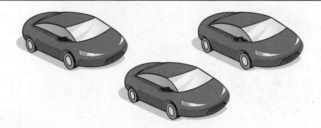 3 cars

 1 pig

 4 pigs

 1 ball

 5 balls

 1 hat

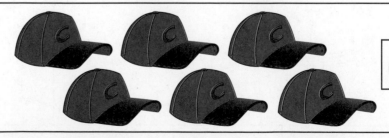 6 hats

1 and More Than 1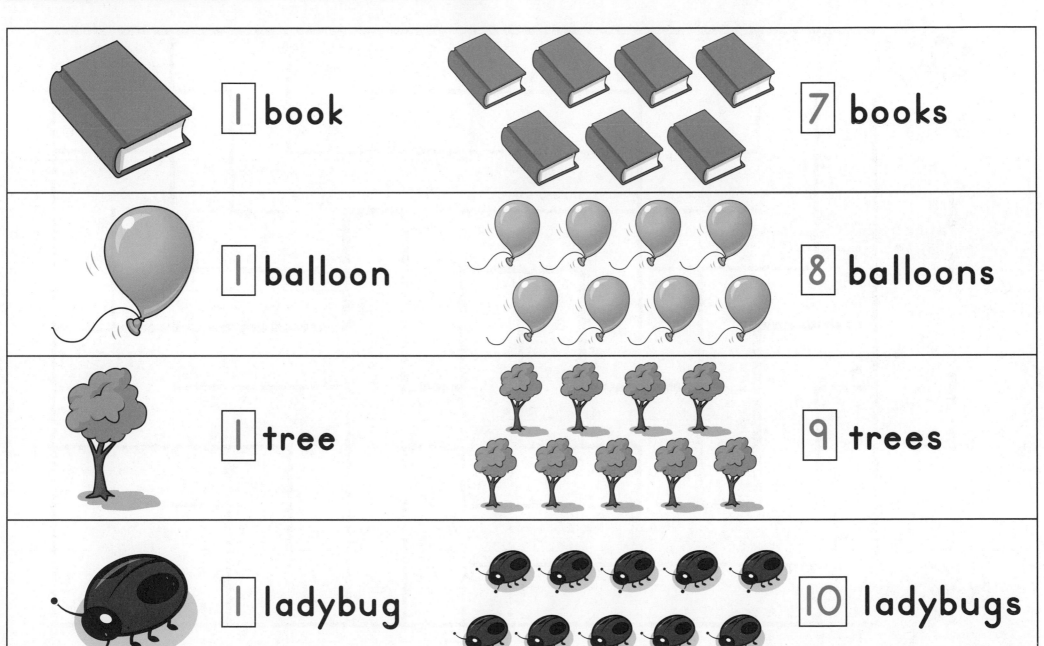

1 book	7 books
1 balloon	8 balloons
1 tree	9 trees
1 ladybug	10 ladybugs

Find Their Homes

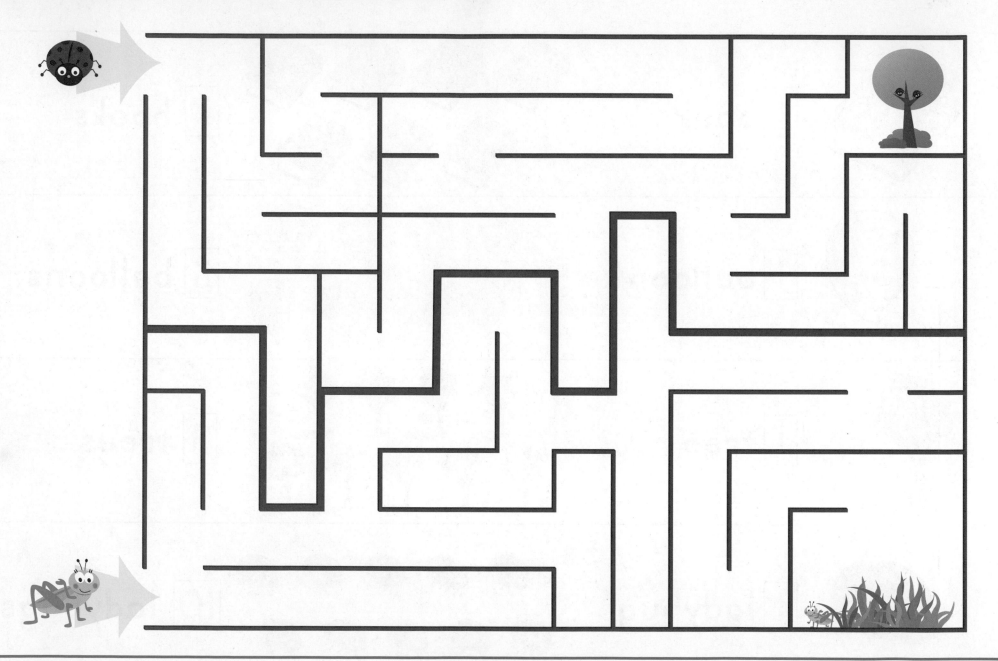

Directions Draw a line from the ladybug to her tree home. Then draw a line from the grasshopper to his home.

My Number and Letter Cards

Name _____